JOHN ORMOND
Selected Poems

POETRY WALES PRESS
1987

POETRY WALES PRESS
56 PARCAU AVENUE, BRIDGEND,
MID GLAMORGAN

© John Ormond, 1987

ISBN 0-907476-73-2

*The publisher acknowledges the financial support of the
Welsh Arts Council*

Cover Design: Jeane Rees
Cover Illustration: 'The Thicket' by Graham Sutherland,
reproduced by kind permission of Mrs Catherine Sutherland
Photograph by Eric Broadbent

Printed in 11 point Garamond

Printed and bound in Great Britain at
The Camelot Press Ltd, Southampton

CONTENTS

I

II

III

IV

V

for Glenys
Rian, Garan and Branwen

The Gift

From where, from whom? Why ask, in torment
All life long when, while we live, we live in it?
As pointless to ask for truth in epiphanies
That throb in the fire, rustle, then fall into ash;
Or why stars are not black in a white firmament.
Enough that it was given, green, as of right, when,
Equally possible, nothing might ever have been.

I

Definition of a Waterfall

Not stitched to air or water but to both
A veil hangs broken in concealing truth

And flies in vague exactitude, a dove
Born diving between rivers out of love

In drums' crescendo beat its waters grow
Conceding thunder's pianissimo

Transfixing ancient time and legend where
A future ghost streams in the present air:

From ledge to pool breakneck across rocks
Wild calm, calm chaos skein their paradox

So that excited poise is fiercely dressed
In a long instant's constant flow of rest,

So that this bridegroom and his bride in white
Parting together headlong reunite

Among her trailing braids. The inconstancy
Is reconciled to fall, falls and falls free

Midwinternight

Midnight chimes at the locks
And the wind wrangles and tangles
The strokes of the country clocks
At the door of the room
Where my child lies calm,
Transfixed in sleep beside her mother.
Under her gentle arm
As sure as silence she shelters
And dreams though the loud dark groans
In the winter of rain and ruin and drums
That thump out tunes with the air's mad bugles.
Still the child sleeps though the village
Rocks on its hinges
And the weathercock changes
His strut every second and screaming
And striding to last on his spiral perch,
That the rain rusts, he spins for a star
That will herald him peace as the gale racks
His heart and the yew breaks.
But she dreams on nothing, and nothing
Will make her stir or cry
From her land of the delicate green trees
And the featherlight sun that stands warm
In her sleep and kind in its sanities.

Her midnight tolls in the flowers and tells
(In a country of descants of harebells
That more than her quiet breath buffets,
Her slightest sigh ruffles and rules)
That the gales cannot charge
Through her eyes with their dirge
And the rain cannot bullet her dream with its rifles.
Yet slowly, slowly, without her murmur or cry
The secret weather that works in to-night
As in all nights and summer, ever and ever,

In her heart though she sleep,
In day though she walk in remotest laughter,
The time that is always with her
Waits for her eyes to awake and raise up
The sun that is kind from its dark;
For her breath, though she die,
To calm the mad strokes of the wind into sleep
And the whole world turn as in blindness
To the green of her far-off trees that grow
To be struck into nearby blossom
And the flower of the carefree country she
By her glance and the children of sleep knows well
As grains of the sand know sea.
So in the country she dwells in she sleeps
And the wind as it is is as nothing,
The clocks out of year and the timed waves
Chiming in air as the still air keeps
Still thunder of graves and wintertime.

Expectation

Waiting that naked figure winged with fire
I know that she will come,
For I have seen her walk from tortuous dream,
Enter the maze and harm of winter,
Each feather flying back
With sulphurous wing-tips spectral flame.

I followed her but lost my way
In the wound woods and suddenly alone,
Dressed in the roping snow,
Tied hard by icy down,
I could not turn to follow or cry
After her, or had I cried
My words would have all been lost
In the curls of the tumbled sky.

Yet where she disappeared
The snowskirl faltered, the ravelling
White waste of the air warmed at her wing
And at her touch a bough
Of a tree burst into green spray,
The incalculable bird began to sing.

I could believe her shape were now
Half dream, half apparition;
For now it is cold, the skies array
Smothering swarms of the snow ready for flight
To silence the world with white.

Birdsong is all a ghost; the thrush
Is silent, unable to relate
How frost falls in her flesh,
Marks her articulate note
With the syllables of cold.
But I await that ghost

Winged with a golden flame;
For at her hands
The wood waves out in wands,
The world finds a new tongue,
Nothing is dumb.
Wind wears the winter's name.
The snow begins to fall. Still she will come.

So sleep, incalculable bird,
No need for flight
Beyond this word
To tell how the world turns.
Whiteness of snow, false morning, though it come,
Though your notes may not touch the sun
They may tell how the sun burns.
Fly towards spring and spring is gone;
Light is elusive as green's secret;
So wait, and sleep; withhold your song
For that moment of the heart's heat
When words break from defeat
And dark and the snow are gone;

When autumn's forced charity,
The brass inevitable coins
That fall from grudging skies
Buy new reasons for the old tunes
That oust the work of snow
And fire the stones to speech,
And the sun's strange eyes
Watch his green aviaries
Shake and bewilder dark
And all light's enemies,
The naked figure loiter through the trees.

Postcard from the Past

Among old bills in a cluttered drawer
I come upon it, wonder why I kept it.
In lese-majesty and love the stamp's
Stuck upside-down. The postmark re-endorses
The name of the resort. Children on rubber horses
Tame the hand-tinted sea. But there is no address

Except my own — an old one — naming a place
Where I am known no longer. Stock phrases
And news of old weather send me a dead greeting.
The final signature is indecipherable.
Nothing makes sense except the final X.

Homage to a Folk-Singer

Phil Tanner, born 1862

This evening is colder, but sit here by the hedge
The first leaves fallen on fire at your feet.
That thrush knows that cold will come. The stones
On the downs will not warm in the sun
Again this summer. This season, autumn, this silence,
Singer, is yours, for an old tune out of the sea.

Turn your face to the channel. Gaze past the headland
Where in the rock silence breeds secret wishes,
Death seeds itself in stone and, set to mark birds down
And their notes, would lock the charmed sea out.

In air and sea bells strike and death runs back
To sleep in the river-bed, the cliff-face:
So silence keeps its place, fixed with a dead shot.

Late? It's too soon for sleep. Past times are up
With us to-night and shake their bells at our bones,
Bury in waves of ringing the step that could sound
On the stair, this, any winter, drown striking clocks
As under the sure frost the sure spring dreams.

Those bells are yours that wave the sea's waves up
To sing of shipwrecks in the bay
And gold that shines like the moon
That lights lovers, love in the green lane.

Do not sleep yet. The tune turns with the wind
For the white sprays of silks and flowers,
Decks dancing weddings, wassails and whistles, brings
Time from the century's grave and furrow, unstops
Old music; and silence, rock, frost, fire, must wait.

*   *   *

Rocks are arrayed, are worked with green
Of weeds that have no words, being of rock.
The sea in our sight is green nearly always;
For it is green at the spine
Of each wave, and fragile blues soon break
With weather. So true sea waters speak
From green for those who sailed or drowned
Down the deep main, whose eyes sea closed,
Salt found, sand settled round
To wind long strands and stories in their brain.

The silent grey of the rocks would prove
That shade outlasts all loves, all lands,
All pure colours of the prism.
But children will clap their hands
For the spring because of the green
That gladdens them at the window-pane
When old men have told them wisely,
"Yes, one more frost is due."
The children do not understand:
"What is the frost but silver?" they demand.
Green is the colour they best know
By dreams of prophecy,
Their careful sleep's experience
And emerald innocence.

They can afford to sleep, being young,
To feed on stuff later years lie about
Saying "Green fails". Black frost is on that tongue.
Age must hold out, keep waking when the eye
Would close its lid perfidiously,
Disprove the stony lie,
And tell of all green sounds that ever rang
When April sprang and girls were garlanding.
I hear them as you sing.

*　　*　　*

Now it is nearly dark. Before we go
Sing as the moon comes up
Of wassailing's white cup
And Henry Martin's story
Of robbing the salt sea, too long ago.

And sing of Fair Phoebe
In a silken gown
With her dark-eyed curly sailor
Whose glance for her was crown.
And for her cruel beauty
Sing, too, of Barbara Allen
Dead in Scarlet Town.

As the moon rises
Sing of the Green Bushes,
The Banks of Primeroses,
Of lovers arm in arm who are gone
To cold, yet who laugh immune
From cold in the long days of a tune.

Sing of every bride for whom
"Green trees the shaded doors did hide".
Bells would have clanged their iron thin
To keep their quiet bodies from the tomb,
From the deep grave, the hands of stone.
But they still ring for true love,
And those figures shall remain:

And look, in moonlight now
They walk with us.
Dancers, lovers, sailors kiss their brides.
O, they are gone now!
But listen hear them cry
Where the long waves ride:
There, suddenly, hear them!
They sing with their hearts' green bells, merrily.

Message in a Bottle

Mariner, the persuasion of the sea
Has worked its sleight of hand again,
Again the horizon's false. So far
Your luck's held out. The sun's come up
Roughly where you expected, has swung
Clockwise in the northern hemisphere.
So far you've kept fair bearings.

But what if I say that suddenly
Beyond that horizon and its horizon too
There is no more land, that after you put out
The meridian altered, all continents fell
Away, sucked down without a blink
Of light or sigh or semaphore?
Suppose I said, "Go sail the seas for an island,
There is none? No reef and no white water
Over coral; nothing but water, that is all your earth?"
That all your change of rigging, the fine
Rejigs to jib, genoa, spinnaker
Are vain, that all you do with the tiller
Will bring you back to nothing,
That even your departure jetty's gone,
That a slow stillness, ghost of a garden's
Fallen upon the lurching of your sea?

You'd shoot the sun again, compose yourself
With old assumptions, trust old courses
On interim charts, find reasons for the silence
On the radio, check your batteries,
Ignore the sinister becalment threatening
Your brain, curse everything before you took
New credence, believe anything rather than believe
Reality had changed, whatever reality is.
Be reassured, I'm talking to myself
And expect no-one to believe me.

But it would be madness to presume
The shore you reach will not be that of a desert,
And madness, too, to suppose that the white dust there
Will not canopy into roses and then yield wheat.

Instructions to Settlers

who arrived in Patagonia from Wales, 1865

On these lean shelves of land
Nothing but thorn thrives.
At noon cross-winds foregather
To suck and subdivide
The dust and the white sand
Between one shelf and another.
With thornstumps then mark out
The plots for your bent lives.
This place is home. Possess
The wilderness with yourselves.
Dig deep. Cut down to zero,
Cut through land's wasted face
To where springs bitter with brine
Pulse sidelong and in vain
Under the restless dust,
Under the windworn plain;
And through the coarsest thorn
Strike with sharp dream, sharp bone
To reach brief union
With this mistaken Canaan.
Search here where seed was lost,
Work stone and white to green.
Ease your tormented ghost.

Finding a Fossil

Maidenhair fern in flint;
An ancient accident
Shows me time's imprint.

A leaf preserved and pressed
Between leaves of stone; crossed
Rest and unrest.

An image that grew green
Took ground in the rock grain:
Dark; now light again.

Luck interlaced each line
And dying vein with stone.
They return to the same sun.

The casual life of fronds,
Air and the tongues of friends;
Green begins, grey ends;

Except that remembered shapes
Live, and that at one's lips
Love speaks as loves lapse.

Graftings (so fused in chance
Among cold stars that dance
Gestures of permanence)

Persist and contrive to invent
From fragment and element
A mindful firmament.

Cathedral Builders

They climbed on sketchy ladders towards God,
With winch and pulley hoisted hewn rock into heaven,
Inhabited sky with hammers, defied gravity,
Deified stone, took up God's house to meet Him,

And came down to their suppers and small beer;
Every night slept, lay with their smelly wives,
Quarrelled and cuffed the children, lied,
Spat, sang, were happy or unhappy,

And every day took to the ladders again;
Impeded the rights of way of another summer's
Swallows, grew greyer, shakier, became less inclined
To fix a neighbour's roof of a fine evening,

Saw naves sprout arches, clerestories soar,
Cursed the loud fancy glaziers for their luck,
Somehow escaped the plague, got rheumatism,
Decided it was time to give it up,

To leave the spire to others; stood in the crowd
Well back from the vestments at the consecration,
Envied the fat bishop his warm boots,
Cocked up a squint eye and said, "I bloody did that".

Michelangelo to Himself, 1550

Forget the Pope, the dead weight of the tomb;
Remember Tuscany and summer.
On hill, in hollow, vineyards yawn awake,
The green wine stretches its arms below Caprese.
Above black cypresses sunlight sucks the grape
And turns the corner of the sky to harvest.
The light is never still, the shade's alive.

Half the madonnas blessing Italy
Gaze into dead dark high upon the walls.
Half the annunciations, crucifixions,
Conceived in day are lost in the church's night
As though to re-witness were to be with the damned.
The church is blind. Only the painters saw them.
The act of making is the act of worship.

Remember the rough, imperfect, constant
Promises of stone. With stubborn chisel
Tenderly bite and ease veins from the marble,
Limbs from the solid block with the soft grain.
Restore, justify shapes in their rightful order.
Startle the light. Let light be thunderstruck
With one more breathing occupant of rock.

The Ambush

after Giovanni Bellini's 'The Assassination of St Peter Martyr'

Ring of black trees, late winter afternoon.
How came this bishop here in the elaborate fish-scales
Of his gold surplice, weighed down, unable to run,
Unable to flee to anywhere in the precise
Enclosing landscape, across the fields to the town
Or into the formality of the far pink hills?
Into the ring of trees wade men with swords.

The mute vermilion sun burns on their blades,
Reveals the fine, explicit, complex branches
On the horizon, every black twig exact;
With its slow falling it levers the horizon up.
The bishop and his attendants drop to their knees.
A slow light snow begins its imprecision
In this particular copse. The saints incur their wounds.
White flowers spring from the ground.

Earlier, woodcutters worked upon this spot,
Now see the tree-stumps bleed
Onto the snow with vegetable compassion
As these martyrs fall and die to rebellious men
Who make the copse a thicket with their spears.

The bloody sun's struck down. The eastern moon comes up.
In the slow beginning snow the saints
Cry out. Dusk, the still afternoon
Surrounds their cries, stifles their blood's music,
Their praise of the unfinished God.

I am the bishop, I am the men with the swords.

After Petrarch

Memories of my youth, my wasted days
Now wound me with regret. Mere mortal things
Enchanted me and chained me, though I had wings
To soar aloft and make men lift their eyes.
O you who witness all my darkest ways,
Invisible God, heaven's almighty king,
Give succour to my soul, frail, wandering
And empty. Come, fill me with your grace:

So that while life was restless as the sea
I'll die calm and in harbour; though I was in vain
I'll journey towards death with honesty.
I pray that in what few short hours remain
To me you'll help me to attain
My hope in you — this the sole hope for me.

To a Nun

after the 15th century Welsh

Please God, forsake your water and dry bread
And fling the bitter cress you eat aside.
Put by your rosary. In Mary's name
Leave chanting creeds to all those monks in Rome.
Spring is at work in woodlands bright with sun;
Springtime's not made for living like a nun.
Your faith, my fairest lady, your religion
Show but a single face of love's medallion.
Slip on this ring and this green gown, these laces;
The wood is furnitured with resting places.
Hide in the birch tree's shade — upon your knees
Murmur the mass of cuckoos, litanies
Of spring's green foliage. There's no sacrilege
If we find heaven here against the hedge.
Remember Ovid's book and Ovid's truth:
There's such a thing as having too much faith.
Let us discover the shapes, the earthly signs
Of our true selves, our souls, among the vines.
For surely God and all his saints above,
High in their other heaven, pardon love.

Landscape without Figures

Cynddylan's hall is dark to-night,
Says the Welsh bard from the days of bows and arrows;
The blood of kinsmen reddened some small rivers,
The singing fool left helpless as usual.

There'd been some battle or other
Fought in a bog, no doubt; as unromantic
And merciless as ever. But fine phrases
Took in charred stones and rafters,
Dead fires under chimneys, benches overturned,
Many men dead out in the dank country.

The old poets were good at this kind of thing;
A bit high-flown, but genuine enough;
Cooking the metre but seldom the reaction.
I know how they felt in the evening wasteland of Wales:
I come upon a farmhouse with old stones tumbling,
The roof fallen-in, nettles at every lintel
And empty cowsheds crumbling, an elder
Loaded with berries and nobody to pick them.
No sign of blood, only tins and broken bottles,
But once lived-in, and now no longer lived-in.

The hall of somebody who was is empty to-night.
But there was a man and his house. It might be said
The elder blossoms each year in token celebration.

Design for a Tomb

Dwell in this stone who once was tenant of flesh.
Alas, lady, the phantasmagoria is over,
Your smile must come to terms with dark for ever.

Carved emblems, puff-cheeked cherubs and full vines,
Buoy up your white memorial in the chapel,
Weightlessly over you who welcomed a little weight.

Lie unprotesting who often lay in the dark,
Once trembling switchback lady keep your stillness
Lest marble crack, ornate devices tumble.

Old melodies were loth to leave your limbs,
Love's deft reluctances where many murmured delight
Lost all their gay glissandi, grew thin and spare

Between a few faint notes. Your bright fever
Turned towards cold, echoed remembered sweets.
Those who for years easily climbed to your casement

Left by the bare front hall. Lust grown respectable
Waltzed slow knight's moves under the portico,
Crabbed in a black gown. You were carried out

Feet first, on your back, still, over the broad chequers.
So set up slender piers, maidenhair stone
Like green fern springing again between ivory oaks,

The four main pillars to your canopy;
And underneath it, up near the cornices
Let in small fenestrations to catch the light.

It still chinks, spy-holing the bent laurel
With worn footholds outside your bedroom window
Through which you'd hear an early gardener's hoe

Chivvy the small weeds on the gravel path
Only to turn dazedly back into your lover's arms,
Fumblingly to doze, calling the morning false.

Lady-lust so arrayed in ornamental bed,
Baring your teeth for the first apple of heaven,
Juices and sap still run. Sleep, well-remembered.

The Hall of Cynddylan

after the Welsh of Llywarch Hên: 9th Century

Cynddylan's hall is dark to-night,
No fire and no bed.
I weep alone, cannot be comforted.

Cynddylan's hall is all in dark to-night,
No fire, no candle-flame:
Whose love, but love of God, can keep me sane?

Cynddylan's hall is dark to-night,
No fire, no gleam of light.
Grief for Cynddylan leaves me desolate.

Cynddylan's hall, its roof is charred and dark,
Such sparkling company sheltered here.
Woe betide him whose whole lot is despair.

Cynddylan's hall, the face of beauty fallen,
He's in his grave who yesterday stood tall.
With him alive no stone fell from the wall.

Cynddylan's hall, forsaken then to-night,
So snatched from his possession.
Death take me so and show me some compassion.

Cynddylan's hall, no safety here to-night,
On Hytwyth's high expanse
No lord, no soldiery, no defence.

Cynddylan's hall is dark to-night,
No fire and no music.
My tears carve out their ravage on my cheeks.

Cynddylan's hall is dark to-night,
No fire, the company's all gone.
My tears tumble down upon its ruin.

Cynddylan's hall, to see it pierces me,
No fire, roof open to the sky:
My lord is dead and here, alive, am I.

Cynddylan's hall, burned to the very ground,
After such comradeship,
Elfan, Cynddylan, Caeawc, all asleep.

Cynddylan's hall, anguish is here to-night.
Once it was held in honour:
Dead are the men and girls who kept it so.

Cynddylan's hall, too much to bear to-night,
Its chieftain lost, O
Merciful God, what can I do?

Cynddylan's hall, the roof is charred and dark
Because the Englishry wreaked havoc on
The pastureland of Elfan and Cynddylan.

Cynddylan's hall is dark to-night,
I mourn Cyndrwynyn's line,
Cynon, Gwiawn and Gwyn.

Cynddylan's hall, my open wound,
After the bustle, all the mirth
I knew upon this hearth.

Saying

Andiamo amigo. We think we see
What we would say. But we lie
Prisoners within those words
We happen to know, captives behind
Bars of arbitrary sound. We grind
Meaning to a halt at the cell wall.

Language, vocabulary, are not the jail
But sounds made ugug, ciphers
That lock one meaning in and exclude
All others. So we express
Exclusive interim reports, construct
A rough equation in makeshift
Habitual sound. We tap on the jail's
Waterpipes, signal through stone
And wait for the vague answer.

So if I say *Areft paradenthic slodan
Aberra antelist mirt maroda*
You say that I say nothing. Though perhaps
I name the god of all green vines;
Or name that process which makes wine
Cloud in the cellar when spring sap climbs
In its far vineyard, but name it
In an inconvenient language not invented,
Or invented once and lost
And now forgotten.

My Dusty Kinsfolk

My dusty kinsfolk in the hill
Screwed up in elm, when you were dead
We tucked you though your hands were still
In the best blanket from your bed
As though you dozed and might in stirring
Push off some light shroud you were wearing.

We did it against double cold,
Cold of your deaths and our own.
We placed you where a vein of coal
Can still be seen when graves are open.
The Dunvant seam spreads fingers in
The churchyard under Penybryn.

And so you lie, my fellow villagers,
In ones and twos and families
Dead behind Ebenezer. Jamjars
Carry flowers for you, but the trees
Put down their roots to you as surely as
You breath was not, and was, and was.

Early and lately dead, each one
Of you haunts me. Continue
To tenant the air where I walk in the sun
Beyond the shadow of yew.
I speak these words to you, my kin
And friends, in requiem and celebration.

Where Home Was

Home was where the glacier long ago
Gouged out the valley; where here
And there the valley's sides cohered
At bridges that had no grace.
They looked the work of men whose blunt
Belief was that a builder's guess,
If good, was better than a long
And bungled calculation.

They clamped together the two halves
Of our village, latchets of smooth
Sandstone coupling the hills.
We lived by one of them, a dingy
Ochre hasp over the branch railway.
Nearby the sidings stretched in smells
Of new pit-props leaking gold glue,
Of smoke and wild chives.

On Sundays when no trains ran
Overnight rain would rust the rails
Except, of course, under the bridges.
We put brown pennies on the silver
Sheltered lines for flattening.
Under our bridge we searched a box
Marked *Private*. In it were oily
Rags, a lantern, an oil-can.

All down the valley the bridges vaulted
The track, mortised and clasped
Good grazing fields to one where the land
Widened and farms straddled the way.
These small frustrated tunnels
Minutely muffled long strands
Of percussive trucks that clanked
In iron staccato under them.

We'd sit on parapets, briefly bandaged
By smoke. The trains went by to town.
We waved our caps to people we'd never
Know. Now it is always Sunday. Weeds
Speed down the line. The bridges
Stand there yet, joists over a green
Nothing. Easier to let them stand
Than ever to pull them down.

Year In, Year Out

By thorn hedges across sharp moonshadow
We climbed to the high farms,
Stumbling in frozen cart-ruts;
Boys beginning to be men,
Saving our words for clear carols.

In nearly-perfect beat, and barely
Breathless, we struck up annunciation
Of the New Year by black gate-posts
Under gabled ricks. Locked-in dogs
Racketed to dismantle the white barns.

Our last rubato notes unbolted
Rhomboids of lamplight into which we walked.
Small round silver warmed our pockets.
Dark beer burned our throats.

Froga

Two yew trees sentried his black garden gate
And every summer Sunday night
He stood between them, a general
Of misery, inspecting them and
The bad joke of the world,

His uniform a black suit, mildew green;
His black velour hat verdigrised round the band
From his sweat at life's jaundice.
His eyebrows were black moustaches,
His moustache the prototype
Of all those worn by practitioners
In the old ambulance books
Where the patient's beyond repair,
But his eyes not evil, rather
The eyes of a dying seal in a bankrupt circus.

Only once did I hear him speak, to scare
Off a blackbird that sang in his yew-tree.
Behind his back we called him Froga,
Half frog, half ogre.

I heard say that they buried him in his suit;
They didn't think it would burn:
And that in his coffin, because they'd taken out
His teeth, he lay there smiling.

Johnny Randall

When the moon was full (my uncle said)
Lunatic Johnny Randall read
The Scriptures in the dead of night
Not in bed by candlelight
But in the field in the silver glow
Across the lane from Howells Row;
And not to himself but to the sheep
With the village barely fallen asleep
And colliers who'd worked two-till-ten
In no fit shape to shout "Amen"
Grumbled "The bugger's off again".

He'd dip in Chronicles and Kings,
Dig into Micah, Obadiah,
Lamentations, Jeremiah,
Ezekiel, Daniel, on and on
Into the Song of Solomon:
A great insomniac heaven-sent
Digest of the Old Testament,
Faltering only in his loud
Recital when a pagan cloud
Darkened the Christian moon and bright
Star congregation of the night.

Then Johnny Randall in a vexed
Improvisation of the text
Would fill in with a few begats
Of Moabs and Jehoshaphats
(Windows banged shut like rifle-shots)
And Azels, Azrikans and all
The genealogy of Saul,
Till David's line put out new shoots
That never sprang from royal roots
And wombs long-barren issued at
The angel seed of Johnny's shouts.

When clouds veered off the moon's clean rim,
Another chapter. Then a hymn
To close the service. So he'd sing

In the big deeps and troughs of sin
No one lifts up my drowning head
Except my bridegroom Jesus Christ
Who on the Cross was crucified...

Then silence. Benediction: *May*
The Love of God and
The Fellowship of the Holy Spirit
Be with you always
Till the great white moon comes again.

Stillness. Until at last
Johnny would rouse himself
And take up collection from the cows.

Organist

Sole village master of the yellowing manual,
And market gardener: his sense of perfect pitch
Took in the cracks between the keys.
He was equipped to hear the tiny discord struck
By any weed which innocently mistook
His garden for a place to grow in.

Five days a week John Owen dug and planted,
Potted and weeded, worried
About Saturday's price in Swansea Market
For his green co-productions with God.

Walking to town at dawn, five miles
With Mary Ann his wife fluting beside him
(She, as they said, would laugh at her own shadow)
With creaking baskets laden, he nearly deafened
Himself with the noise of his own boots.

Sabbath, inside the spade-sharp starch
Of his crippling collar, he husbanded
On the harmonium aged couplers
And celestes into a grave, reluctant
Order; took no heed in the hymns
Of the congregation trailing a phrase behind,
Being intent and lost in the absolute beat.

But, with the years, philosopher as he was,
A Benthamite of music, he set more store
By the greatest harmony of the greatest number.
When, pentecostal, guilts were flung away
Fortissimo from pinnacles of fervour,
When all were cleansed of sin in wild
Inaccurate crescendoes of Calvary,
Uncaring, born again, dazzled by diadems
In words of a Jerusalem beyond their lives,

The choristers would stray from the safe fold
Of the true notes. John Owen would transpose
By half a tone in the middle of the hymn
To disguise the collective error,
But sure of the keys of his own kingdom.

He lies long since in counterpoint
With a few stones of earth; is beyond any doubt
The one angel of the village cloud
Who sings from old notation;
The only gardener there whose cocked ear
Can discern the transgression, the trespass
Of a weed into the holy fields,
If there are weeds in heaven.

My Grandfather and his Apple Tree

Life sometimes held such sweetness for him
As to engender guilt. From the night vein he'd come,
From working in water wrestling the coal,
Up the pit slant. Every morning hit him
Like a journey of trams between the eyes;
A wild and drinking farmboy sobered by love
Of a miller's daughter and a whitewashed cottage
Suddenly to pay rent for. So he'd left the farm
For dark under the fields six days a week
With mandrel and shovel and different stalls.
All light was beckoning. Soon his hands
Untangled a brown garden into neat greens.

There was an apple tree he limed, made sturdy;
The fruit was sweet and crisp upon the tongue
Until it budded temptation in his mouth.
Now he had given up whistling on Sundays,
Attended prayer-meetings, added a concordance
To his wedding Bible and ten children
To the village population. He nudged the line,
Clean-pinafored and collared, glazed with soap,
Every seventh day of rest in Ebenezer;
Shaved on a Saturday night to escape the devil.

The sweetness of the apples worried him.
He took a branch of cooker from a neighbour
When he became a deacon, wanting
The best of both his worlds. Clay from the colliery
He thumbed about the bole one afternoon
Grafting the sour to sweetness, bound up
The bleeding white of junction with broad strips
Of working flannel-shirt and belly-bands
To join the two in union. For a time
After the wound healed the sweetness held,
The balance tilted towards an old delight.

But in the time that I remember him
(His wife had long since died, I never saw her)
The sour half took over. Every single apple
Grew — across twenty Augusts — bitter as wormwood.
He'd sit under the box tree, his pink gums
(Between the white moustache and goatee beard)
Grinding thin slices that his jack-knife cut,
Sucking for sweetness vainly. It had gone,
Gone. I heard him mutter
Quiet Welsh oaths as he spat the gall-juice
Into the seeding onion-bed, watched him toss
The big core into the spreading nettles.

Full-Length Portrait of a Short Man

A good fat sheep, unsheared, could have bolted
Between Will Bando's legs. They made such a hoop,
Clipping his hips to the ground,
I thought he'd been a jockey. He had the gait,
The boy's body. He strutted with careful
Nonchalance, past the five village shops
We somehow called The Square, on the outside
Edges of his hand-stitched boots, punishing
The bracket of his thigh with a stripped twig.
But he'd have slipped round on a horse
Like a loose saddle-band.

                     In fact, he'd been a tailor;
From boyhood sat so long cross-legged,
Picking, re-picking his needle as though piercing
Points of dust, his sewing hand conducting
The diminishing slow movement of silko into seam,
That his legs bent and stayed bent. His years were spent
Coaxing smooth drapes for praying shoulders
Humbled on soft-named farms, stitching Sunday-best
For the small Atlases who, six days every week,
Held up the owners' world in the colliery's
Wet headings. His box-pleats in black serge adorned
The preacher proffering the great reward.

Will Bando ate perpetual cold meat
At his life's table: doomed bachelor, burdened
With thirst as might have burned his natural
Good grace; though drink increased his courtesy.
He'd tip his hat twice to the same lady,
Apologize to walls he fell against,
Pat on the head short bushes that he brushed by.
The needle's eye of village approbation
Was wide to this certain thread. But drunk,
On a dark night, his welcome was a door locked

Early against him by his lank and grudging sister.
He'd doss down in the woodshed on clean sticks.

One Sunday, deep in the thrust of red weather
Wounding October, Will was in no rick or woodshed
We could find. He'd strayed before. But Monday came
And our feet snagged paths in the morning cambric
Of frost on field after field. Every hedge and dingle
Beaten, every crony questioned, gave echoes back
As answers. Days drifted him away. In vain we cried
Into the last derelict barn, hamlets, hills distant.
The evening paper in the market town
Printed our picture silently shouting;
And one of Will from an old snapshpot with a stranger's
Smile badly re-touched to a false line.

                  Children at fox and hounds found him.
He lay in the broken air-shaft, twenty years disused,
Of the shut and festering pit, not half a mile
From home. Rubble and tumbled bricks
Gave him sanctuary. Fallen where an unended
Dream of shelter brought him, he had given death
'Good Evening'. His hat with orange feather
At the brim was in his hand. He wore his smart
Fawn herring-bone with the saddle-stitch lapels.

Tombstones

Inscriptions, ritual statements
Of time's imbalance, of resources
Drained from the bank of seasons,
Painfully tell us nothing. In due course
The stonemason's phraseology will tap
Its short syllables into the skull.

Could you spell out
At death's precise dictation
A three-line version of your own life?
Could you say more in less
At half-a-crown a cut letter?

Lichens censor all but the primitive
Incisions of arbitrary dates.
Ochre elisions, encrustations
Blur the clean granite lines
Of most lives set down here.

Epitaph for Uncle Johnnie

Here lies a tenor. For his grace rejoice.
His soaring notes rang out, the rafters rang.
He gave God glory with his golden voice
And lived the silver music that he sang.

At his Father's Grave

Here lies a shoemaker whose knife and hammer
Fell idle at the height of summer,
Who was not missed so much as when the rain
Of winter brought him back to mind again.

He was no preacher but his working text
Was *See all dry this winter and the next.*
Stand still. Remember his two hands, his laugh,
His craftsmanship. They are his epitaph.

After a Death

Come back to the house, I turn the key in the door,
Pull back the curtains to let out the dark,
Kindle a fire, wind up my grandfather's clock,
Then see the slug's trail on the kitchen floor.

I have inherited him with all the rest
Of whatever's here, the pictures, the jugs, the beds
Nobody sleeps in any more. Presumably he feeds
On something here. He wouldn't come for dust.

The tables and chairs are mine, the brass trinket box,
White plates that write their O's across the dresser,
The coats and shoes in cupboards, the old letters,
The pots, the pans, the towels, the knives and forks,

The small effects of other people's lives,
— And him who wasn't mentioned in the will
Who entered from the garden once and still
From time to time inspects his territory then leaves.

A list's a list and offers me no order,
I see the silver trail, know other presences.
A death's a death. I mourn three absences.
If I wait here they'll speak when time is older.

The Key

Its teeth worked doubtfully
At the worn wards of the lock,
Argued half-heartedly
With the lock's fixed dotage.
Between them they deferred decision.
One would persist, the other
Not relent. That lock and key
Were old when Linus Yale
Himself was born. Theirs
Was an ageless argument.

The key was as long as my hand,
The ring of it the size
Of a girl's bangle. The bit
Was inches square. A grandiose key
Fit for a castle, yet our terraced
House was two rooms up, two down;
Flung there by sullen pit-owners
In a spasm of petulance, discovering
That colliers could not live
On the bare Welsh mountain:

Like any other house in the domino
Row, except that our door
Was nearly always on the latch.
Most people just walked in, with
'Anybody home?' in greeting
To the kitchen. This room
Saw paths of generations cross;
This was the place to which we all came
Back to talk by the oven, on the white
Bench. This was the home patch.

And so, if we went out, we hid
The key — though the whole village

Knew where it was — under a stone
By the front door. We lifted up
The stone, deposited the key
Neatly into its own shape
In the damp earth. There, with liquid
Metal, we could have cast,
Using that master mould,
Another key, had we had need of it.

Sometimes we'd dip a sea-gull's
Feather in oil, corkscrew it
Far into the keyhole to ease
The acrimony there. The feather, askew
In the lock, would spray black
Droplets of oil on the threshold
And dandruff of feather-barb.
The deep armoreal stiffness, tensed
Against us, stayed. We'd put away
The oil, scrub down the front step.

The others have gone for the long
Night away. The evidence of grass
Re-growing insists on it. This time
I come back to dispose of what there is.
The knack's still with me. I plunge home
The key's great stem, insinuate
Something that was myself between
The two old litigants. The key
Engages and the bolt gives to me
Some walls enclosing furniture.

Paraphrase for Edwin Arlington Robinson

It was Sod's Law and not the sun
That made things come unstuck for Icarus.

The same applies to all with a seeming head
For heights, a taste for the high wires,

Flatulent aerialists who burped
At the critical moment then fell akimbo

In a tattered arc, screaming, down
Out of the illusion, the feathery Eden.

So when your mother died of black diphtheria
And neither quack nor priest would call

To give their pince-nezed ministrations,
You and your brothers wrung cold compresses

In vain for her wild brow, cleft her grave
Yourselves, thumped clods on her plank coffin.

Later one brother took to drink and drugs.
The other slotted the family investments

Into curt bankruptcy. Meanwhile your father
Tried coaxing ghosts. Table-tappings

Stuttered perniciously from the next room
To yours, harangued your shuttering deafness.

Sometimes you imagined you detected clues
To a code, but it was only the singing wires

Of the death of the aural, the eighth nerve
Shrinking from lack of blood. That fenced you

High on a dangerous peak of vertigo, giddy
But unfalling. You said you mourned a "lost

Imperial music". What you were emperor of
Was a domain you did not recognize

As worth the name: a kingdom of aspirers
Without wings, a thin parish of prophets

Without words — except for baffled Amen,
A scraggy choir without a common hymn,

But no man without music in the throng
And each man sawing at his own bleak tune.

Letter to a Geologist

for Wynn Williams

When was it we last met? When the stag
Devoured the vivid serpent then wept
Jewels as tears, antidote to all poisons.

Or so it seems to me. You write
Of your November find, fossil coral
Within a spit of that house of yours

(Which is too far from me. The free hold
Of our friendship is at stake); the coral,
Bring me a piece of it, bring it soon.

I would place it with that other handful
Torn, only last year, from a living reef
Six thousand miles away in the Indian Ocean;

And, in the pairing, see what you deduce:
That once your Flintshire hill — for me as distant
As the Seychelles themselves — was tropical.

The shifting land you've shown me: off-shore
Islands in green counties; tide-ways
500 million years of age under the plough;

And desert sands stranded in river-cliffs
On Deeside, come from the Sahara.
If these could move, could not *you* move, too?

Come south. Ferns in grey shale speak of you
From my shelf, of coal measures we were both
Born on. Your nugget of fool's gold

Is paperweight over the dross of my draft poems.
I know that, as I greet you, mountains shrink
Or inch up; the sea-kings' beds are unmade;

But these are rustlings, mere cosmic sighs
Unheard beneath our breathing. Let us tell
Some part of earth's true time together soon

With a drink, a song — the lullabies you sang
My children, come sing them again before sleep;
Let us say to each other words of a common world.

I've grown too solemn, so recall your jest
Of Man's not really falling off the peg
Vertical, ready-made, in Genesis:

But should you, in the field, come upon Moses
Striding through cloud on a Snowdonian height
With new or adjusted Tablets of the Law

Please check the Lord's amendments
Before you raise your hammer to opine
What stone it is that they are carved upon.

Yours, as the mountains move,
                            Love, ever,
                                    John.

Lament for a Leg

Near the yew tree under which the body of Dafydd ap Gwilym is buried in Strata Florida, Cardiganshire, there stands a stone with the following inscription: 'The left leg and part of the thigh of Henry Hughes, Cooper, was cut off and interr'd here, June 18, 1756'. Later the rest of Henry Hughes set off across the Atlantic in search of better fortune.

A short service, to be sure,
With scarcely half a hymn they held,
Over my lost limb, suitable curtailment.
Out-of-tune notes a crow cawed
By the yew tree, and me,
My stump still tourniquèd,
Awkward on my new crutch,
Being snatched towards the snack
Of a funeral feast they made.
With seldom a dry eye, for laughter,
They jostled me over the ale
I'd cut the casks for, and the mead.
"Catch me falling under a coach",
Every voice jested, save mine,
Henry Hughes, cooper. A tasteless caper!
Soon with my only, my best, foot forward
I fled, quiet, to far America:

Where, with my two tried hands, I plied
My trade and, true, in time made good
Though grieving for Pontrhydfendigaid.
Sometimes, all at once, in my tall cups,
I'd cry in *hiraeth* for my remembered thigh
Left by the grand yew in Ystrad Fflur's
Bare ground, near the good bard.
Strangers, astonished at my high
Beer-flush, would stare, not guessing,
Above the bar-board, that I, of the starry eye,
Had one foot in the grave; thinking me,

64

No doubt, a drunken dolt in whom a whim
Warmed to madness, not knowing a tease
Of a Welsh worm was tickling my distant toes.

"So I bequeath my leg", I'd say and sigh,
Baffling them, "my unexiled part, to Dafydd
The pure poet who, whole, lies near and far
From me, still pining for Morfudd's heart",
Giving him, generous to a fault
With what was no more mine to give,
Out of that curt plot, my quarter grave,
Good help, I hope. What will the great God say
At Dafydd's wild-kicking-climbing extra leg,
Jammed hard in heaven's white doorway
(I'll limp unnimble round the narrow back)
Come the quick trumpet of the Judgement Day?

III

In September

Again the golden month, still
Favourite, is renewed;
Once more I'd wind it in a ring
About your finger, pledge myself
Again, my love, my shelter,
My good roof over me,
My strong wall against winter.

Be bread upon my table still
And red wine in my glass; be fire
Upon my hearth. Continue,
My true storm door, continue
To be sweet lock to my key;
Be wife to me, remain
The soft silk on my bed.

Be morning to my pillow,
Multiply my joy. Be my rare coin
For counting, my luck, my
Granary, my promising fair
Sky, my star, the meaning
Of my journey. Be, this year too,
My twelve months long desire.

Cat's Cradles

We shape string patterns, each design
   crossing from hand to hand
   between us as we play.
So, with light touch,
   your fingertips meet mine.
   You lift this loop then that
to intertwine and weave them
   backwards and forwards.
   You see that no stray tangles,
no accidents to design
   snag the game's progress.
   Intent, closer our heads incline;
your hair touches my face;
   between your lips I see
   the tip of your tongue's stillness.
Now, serious popinjay,
   when with light touch
   your fingertips meet mine
I grow impatient
   wishing to consign
   more than mere string to you.

Soon I relay
   adroit reciprocations
   of design less than adroitly;
and you insist this shrine
   of cord be finished first.
   What can I say
(again that touch, your fingertips at mine)
   except "Be quick, be careless.
   Forget these fine
adjustments to the thread.
   Why not mislay one strand
   and let all ravel and slackly run?"
So that elsewhere, nearby,

I shall not sigh impatience
    but breathe the air you exhale
when softly you design
    (your calm undone)
    how next you move,
when, with an even lighter touch,
    your fingertips and lips
        silence me, and consent, in meeting mine.

Design for a Quilt

First let there be a tree, roots taking ground
In bleached and soft blue fabric.
Into the well-aired sky branches extend
Only to bend away from the turned-back
Edge of linen where day's horizons end;

Branches symmetrical, not over-flaunting
Their leaves (let ordinary swansdown
Be their lining), which in the summertime
Will lie lightly upon her, the girl
This quilt's for, this object of designing;

But such too, when deep frosts veneer
Or winds prise at the slates above her,
Or snows lie in the yard in a black sulk,
That the embroidered cover, couched
And applied with pennants of green silk,

Will still be warm enough that should she stir
To draw a further foliage about her
The encouraged shoots will quicken
And, at her breathing, midnight's spring
Can know new season as they thicken.

Feather-stitch on every bough
A bird, one neat French-knot its eye,
To sing a silent night-long lullaby
And not disturb her or disbud her.
See that the entwining motives run

In and about themselves to bring
To bed the sheens and mossy lawns of Eden;
For I would have a perfect thing
To echo if not equal Paradise
As garden for her true temptation:

So that in future times, recalling
The pleasures of past falling, she'll bequeath it
To one or other of the line,
Bearing her name or mine,
With luck I'll help her make beneath it.

Summer Mist

Branches have common tenancy
Arrangements, moving in and out
Of one another's air at the wind's
Say-so. Where their top joints belong
Is never clear-cut:

Except as when hiatus calm of August
Forestalls September. Then mist
The silencer happens into grey,
Mist variously impaled upon the land
Subtracts the pulse of colour.

On such a windless day two men, their
Voices ravelling its few hours, gave
And gave way in words. Easily
They could have sung together.
They knew each other's unsung tunes.

Dusk and the mist closed on them
In the last lane. Now one instructs
The other: "Remember that the wind
Will soon return, remember
You are welcome to my air".

Certain Questions for Monsieur Renoir

Did you then celebrate
That grave discovered blue
With salt thrown on a fire
In honour of all blues?

I mean the dress of La Parisienne
(Humanly on the verge of the ceramic),
Blue of Delft, dream summary of blues,
Centre-piece of a fateful exhibition;

Whose dress-maker and, for that matter,
Stays-maker the critics scorned;
Who every day receives her visitors
In my country where the hard slate is blue.

She has been dead now nearly a century
Who wears that blue of smoke curling
Beyond a kiln, and blue of gentians,
Blue of lazurite, turquoise hauled

Over the blue waves, blue water, from Mount Sinai;
Clematis blue: she, Madame Henriot,
Whose papers fall to pieces in the files
In the vaults of the Registrar General.

Did you see in her garment the King of Illyria
Naming his person's flower in self-love?
And in the folds, part of polyphony
Of all colour, thunder blue,

Blue of blue slipper-clay, blue
Of the blue albatross? Blue sometimes
Without edge, blue liquified
By distance? Or did they start

Those ribbons at her wrists in blue
Of a sea-starwort? Or in verdigris, perhaps,
Blue on a Roman bead? Or in that regal blue
Of the Phoenicians, of boiled whelks;

That humbly-begun but conquering blue
Which, glowing, makes a god of man?
She who is always poised between appointments
For flirtation, what nuances of blue

Her bodice had, this blue you made
For your amusement, painter of fans and porcelain,
You set on gaiety; who saw, in the blue fog
Of the city, a candle burning blue

(Not heralding a death but) harbouring
A clear illusion, blue spot on the young salmon,
A greater blue in shadow; blue's calm
Insistence on a sense. Not for you

Indigo blue, or blue of mummy's cloth
Or the cold unction of mercury's blue ointment,
But the elect blue of love in constancy,
Blue, true blue, blue gage, blue plum,

Blue fibrils of a form, roundness
Absorbed by light, quintessence
Of blue beautiful. It was not blue
Tainted, taunted by dark. Confirm it.

The eyes are bells to blue
Inanimate pigment set alight
By gazing which was passionate.
So what is midnight to this midinette?

Ultramarine, deep-water blue?
Part of a pain and darkness never felt?
Assyrian crystal? Clouded blue malachite?

Blue of a blue dawn trusting light.

Captive Unicorn

His bones are red from lady's bedstraw.
He is fed, too, according to season,
Dry meadow-rue, juiceless rest-harrow.

Enchanter's nightshade made him docile.
He was led abject, pathetic
In jewelled collar, into this palisade.

The stains on his flanks are not of blood;
The bursting pomegranates spill their seeds
From the tree where he's tethered.

He day-dreams of jack-by-the-hedge, lances
Of goldenrod to crunch on, tangled
Heart's ease, salads of nipple-wort.

His nightmares are acres of fool's parsley.
He wakes hungry for self-heal
And the clingings of traveller's joy.

Released in winter, he does not stray.
The tip of his horn a blind periscope,
He trembles in sweet dung under deep snow.

Night in a Hundred

Cantre'r Gwaelod

Everywhere revellers, wassailers,
In a real spectacular; and surly
Beyond the wall, the devious sea,
That other great leveller.

Out in the midnight air, sleepless
With gripe, the town's teetotaller
Heard what he took to be voices
Crying, over the water, of vengeance.

He tried talking the rest into sense.
They ordered more wine to be brought.
Ashen of pallor, the servant returned
With a tale of fish in the cellar.

But glasses were recharged. The harper
Was made to play, over again,
The same old tunes of victories
Which had always been meaningless.

The company, maudlin and drooling,
Tottering from pillar to pillar,
Slewed off to bed, slurring and reeling.
Then the chairs floated up to the ceiling.

All round the town the scenes had been
Similar; guzzlers in every parlour,
The sea lapping at their squalor.
In came the hungriest roller.

At dawn there was only the blank acreage
Of the sea, with the harp drifting on it;
The stuff of a new sad song
Which proved to be popular.

The Birth of Venus at Aberystwyth

Beyond the pier varicose waves crocheted
A complex permanent nothing on the stones.
The Corporation deck-chairs flapped
Haphazard unison. Most sea-front windows

Confessed to Vacancies; and on the promenade
A violinist in Scotch-plaid dinner-jacket
Contributed little to the Welsh way of life
As he played 'Thanks for the Memory'

To two small children and a dog. Without
Any expectation at all, the sea brandished
Its vanity. The one-eyed coastguard was dozing.
Nothing in the sky sought a response.

The occasional pebble moved, gave itself back
To the perpetual, casual disorder
Of all perfectly-shaped, meaningless forms,
Like pebbles. There was one beachcomber,

From Basingstoke, but he noticed nothing
Unusual either when far out, beyond
The beginning of the ninth (one could even
Go as far as to say the ninetieth) wave,

Dolphins who hadn't spoken to each other
For years formed squadrons for her.
Trenches of water broke open, deep
Where she was, coming up. Weeds fandangoed,

Currents changed their course. Inside
An instant's calm her hair began to float,
Marbling the hollows like old ledgers.
The sea still tells the story in its own

Proud language, but few understand it;
And, as you may imagine, the beauty of it is lost
In the best translations available...
Her different world was added to the world

As, nearing shore, sensing something dubious,
Something fishy in the offing, the dolphin-fleet
Turned back. The lady nearly drowned,
But hobbled in, grazing her great toe.

Do not ask questions about where she came from
Or what she was, or what colour was her hair;
Though there are reasons for supposing
That, when it dried, its light took over

Where the summer left off. The following Sunday
She wore a safe beige hat for morning service
At the Baptist Church. Even so, the minister
Ignored her as she left, and she didn't go again.

Castiglion Fiorentino

Given luck, not that such given luck
Is ever likely to bring one back
To see again what once one saw:

Here, although it is night, a near plain
With foothills breathing deep beyond, and
In the foreground eight nearly absolute

Arches, though the stone crumbles here
And there from warm geometries of sandstone,
Definitions of stillness beyond, the never-sleeping

Of cypresses and a prospect of calm
That the heart hungers for and the heart
Stops at, that is, if this is the place.

It is night, and there's no certainty.
With luck the landscape will lie climbing
Into beneficence of green, each gesture

Of land giving back the sun. There will be
No way back from its almost perfection, no way
To find its other version, except she were here.

For Glenys

To tell you something I've discovered,
This letter from a land too far from you.
Believe, if you so wish, that the same
Distance exists between two persons
Or two points. It is not so.

I am further from you than you could guess
From the scale of a map or such weak
Atlases as we possess. By some inverted
Theorem of love I should be next to you.
But gentle loins and pitiless leagues apart

Prove me the converse. Old standards
And numbers are changed by the price of bucket-shop
Air-tickets, the stand-by flights of geography
And fancy. How, I wonder, having travelled
Without you, could loneliness cost less?

The far blessing is that not nonetheless
But more than less I love you; and discover
That perhaps we've been together for so long
That what my greatest need is is to be
If not quite with you, then in the next room

To you so that I hear you reply to some query
Even about a bill (though such questions,
You know, too well, are not exactly my style);
To prove that we are still the lovers that we were,
At war with death, its notions, and all bad weather.

Note from Cortona

Three o'clock. The small city soundless. Below,
A hundred tipsy roofs of medieval cards
Collapse towards the plain; but lightened now
Of their feather-weight of swifts skimming and nesting,
Might just survive another winter snowfall.
Two or three friends ask of you every day.

And each and cloudless morning I climb up
By the broken flagstone path where the vines,
Pleating the mountainside together, make slow
Melodies on its patient staves; the sweet peas
Gone, the blue moths' colour darkened
Into the elder. To-day at our stone table

I raised a glass to you. The sunflowers
Harvested, the haws scarlet as sunset,
I came down by the steep Etruscan way
Where the wind has flattened the wild white wheat
By the yellow cacti that are brown now;
When will their sisters flower in your garden?

I shall come home past St Mary's-by-the-Limepit
That the shoemakers erected, wondering
If that's one reason I return so often
To this high balcony of earth. In guilty absence
I greet you, and with a love
That's sharpened by my love of this dear place.

Elsewhere

My wife tells me I snore. The night long
(To me it's hearsay, having been elsewhere)
She has played at in-and-out-the-windows
Of her poor sleep's tenement while I all industry
Felled an adjacent forest with my chainsaw.

I hear her dark-before-dawn report, and try
To stay awake in separate neighbourhood
To give her a head start towards the wood
That she would enter too — but quietly —
Patient upon the path her patience leads to.

Who is she when she is gone? In what season
Does she wander, under what leaves? What words
Does she utter before she returns, herself
Upon her waking, when what is not has contracted
To my discovered side in the warm bed?

Time to be up. The essence of who and what
Is mere quibble by easy labour of sunlight
Rebuttressing the bedroom walls so soon.
But a branch's wraith of shadow on the ceiling,
The question's ever-presence, clenches and trembles.

IV

Ancient Monuments

for Alexander Thom

They bide their time off serpentine
Green lanes, in fields, with railings
Round them and black cows; tall, pocked
And pitted stones, grey, ochre-patched
With moss, lodgings for lost spirits.

Sometimes you have to ask their
Whereabouts. A bent figure, in a hamlet
Of three houses and a barn, will point
Towards the moor. You find them there,
Aloof lean markers, erect in mud.

Long Meg, Five Kings, Nine Maidens,
Twelve Apostles: with such familiar names
We make them part of ordinary lives.
On callow pasture-land
The Shearers and The Hurlers stand.

Sometimes they keep their privacy
In public places: nameless, slender slabs
Disguised as gate-posts in a hedge; and some,
For centuries on duty as scratching-posts,
Are screened by ponies on blank uplands.

Search out the farthest ones, slog on
Through bog, bracken, bramble: arrive
At short granite footings in a plan
Vaguely elliptical, alignments sunk
In turf strewn with sheep's droppings;

And wonder whether it was this shrunk place
The guide-book meant, or whether
Over the next ridge the real chamber,

Accurate by the stars, begins its secret
At once to those who find it.

Turn and look back. You'll see horizons
Much like the ones that they saw,
The tomb-builders, milleniums ago;
The channel scutched by rain, the same old
Sediment of dusk, winter returning.

Dolerite, porphyry, gabbro fired
At the earth's young heart: how those men
Handled them. Set on back-breaking
Geometry, the symmetries of solstice,
What they awaited we, too, still await.

Looking for something else, I came once
To a cromlech in a field of barley.
Whoever farmed that field had true
Priorities. He sowed good grain
To the tomb's doorstep. No path

Led to the ancient death. The capstone,
Set like a cauldron on three legs,
Was marooned by the swimming crop.
A gust and the cromlech floated,
Motionless at time's moorings.

Hissing dry sibilance, chafing
Loquacious thrust of seed
This way and that, in time and out
Of it, would have capsized
The tomb. It stayed becalmed.

The bearded foam, rummaged
By wind from the westerly sea-track,
Broke short not over it. Skirted

By squalls of that year's harvest,
That tomb belonged in that field.

The racing barley, erratically-bleached
Bronze, cross-hatched with gold
And yellow, did not stop short its tide
In deference. It was the barley's
World. Some monuments move.

Salmon

first for, and now in memory of, Ceri Richards

The river sucks them home.
The lost past claims them.
  Beyond the headland
It gropes into the channel
Of the nameless sea.
  Off-shore they submit
To the cast, to the taste of it.
It releases them from salt,
Their thousand miles in odyssey
For spawning. It rehearsed their return
  From the beginning; now
  It clenches them like a fist.

The echo of once being here
Possesses and inclines them.
  Caught in the embrace
Of nothing that is not now,
Riding in with the tide-race,
  Not by their care,
Not by any will they know,
They turn fast to the caress
Of their only course. Sea-hazards done,
They ache towards the one world
  From which their secret
  Sprang, perpetuate

More than themselves, the ritual
Claim of the river, pointed
  Towards rut, tracing
Their passion out. Weeping philosopher,

They reaffirm the world,
   The stars by which they ran,
Now this precise place holds them
Again. They reach the churning wall
Of the brute waterfall which shed
Them young from its cauldron pool.
   A hundred times
   They lunge and strike

Against the hurdles of the rock;
Though hammering water
   Beats them back
Still their desire will not break.
They flourish, whip and kick,
   Tensile for their truth's
Sake, give to the miracle
Of their treadmill leaping
The illusion of the natural.
The present in torrential flow
   Nurtures its own
   Long undertow:

They work it, strike and streak again,
Filaments in suspense.
   The lost past shoots them
Into flight, out of their element,
In bright transilient sickle-blades
   Of light; until upon
The instant's height of their inheritance
They chance in descant over the loud
Diapasons of flood, jack out of reach
And snatch of clawing water,
   Stretch and soar
   Into easy rapids

Beyond, into half-haven, jounce over
Shelves upstream; and know no question
    But, pressed by their cold blood,
Glance through the known maze.
They unravel the thread to source
    To die at their ancestry's
Last knot, knowing no question.
They meet under hazel trees,
Are chosen, and so mate. In shallows as
The stream slides clear yet shirred
    With broken surface where
    Stones trap the creamy stars

Of air, she scoops at gravel with fine
Thrust of her exact blind tail;
    At last her lust
Gapes in a gush on her stone nest
And his held, squanderous peak
    Shudders his final hunger
On her milk; seed laid on seed
In spunk of liquid silk.
So in exhausted saraband their slack
Convulsions wind and wend galactic
    Seed in seed, a found
    World without end.

The circle's set, proportion
Stands complete, and,
    Ready for death,
Haggard they hang in aftermath
Abundance, ripe for the world's
    Rich night, the spear.
Why does this fasting fish
So haunt me? Gautama, was it this
You saw from river-bank

At Uruvela? Was this
  Your glimpse
  Of holy law?

Tricephalos

The first face spoke: Under sheep-run
And mole-mound and stifling glade
I was awake though trapped in the mask

Of dirt. Counting the centuries,
I scrutinized the void, but its question
Stared me out. What was it I remembered

As, above me in the world, generation
Upon futile generation of tall trees,
Forest after forest, grew and fell?

It was that once the ease, the lease
Of a true spring saw my brow decked
With sprigs, my gaze complete and sensual.

My eyes (the second said) were fixed
In hunger for the whole regard
Of what might be, the god beyond the god.

Time and again the black loam blazed
And shuddered with false auguries.
Passionless, vigilant, I kept faith,

Invented systems, sounds, philosophies
In which some far, long-listened-for,
Long-perfect melody might thrive.

The imagined dropped away, the perfect
Knew no advent. My sight was lost in sleep
And that stone sleep was haunted.

Two living garlands (spoke the third)
Strove to be one inside our common skull.
They half-entwined the unavailing dreams

96

Fashioned from light that is and words
That seemed ours for the saying.
I await wisdom wise enough to know

It will not come. The inaccessible song
Upon whose resolution we, awake, expectant,
Yearning for order, lie, is the one tune

That we were born for. Its cadence
Shapes our vision and our blindness.
The unaccountable is my stone smile.

Winter Rite

Mother-of-pearl in cloud, the sun low
Over the holy island; the straggle
Of sacred timber flexed and crook-back
For the dark months' long assailment;
And the lake where the god sprawls
Sleeping under rotted water-lilies, weed
Clogged at his groin.
       Safe fish weave basketries
Of bubbles through his fingers.
Year in, year out, in this wan season
We bring him offerings: spears, axes,
Sickle-blades, bronze scoops and bridle bits.

We have given him prisoners
For his drowned army, their screams at the knife
Sleep-songs for his still warriorship.
He is a god, he knows our service.

We have taken the great boar live
Then cast it into his pool, fenced it
With sacrificial arrows. It threshed
Until it died for his fresh food.

Year after year before the god's lake freezes
We climb to his stone altars. They tilt
Above the lilies which were gold in summer.
We face, despite our fears,
The god's invisible three faces.
       We do not expect to see him.
He allows us to approach and accepts our gifts
With the silence of all gods.

Landscape in Dyfed

for Graham Sutherland

Because the sea grasped cleanly here, and there
Coaxed too unsurely until clenched strata
Resisted, an indecision of lanes resolves
This land into gestures of beckoning
Towards what is here and beyond, and both at hand.

Walk where you will, below is an estuary.
In advance to a fleeting brightness you traverse
So many shoals of the dead who have drowned
In stone, so many hibernations
Of souls, you could be in phantom country.

But the tapers of gorse burn slowly, otherwise.
And here are rock cathedrals which can be
As small as your span. And, at the water's edge,
A struck havoc of trees clutches the interim season,
The given roots bare, seeming to feed on the wind;

And in their limbs what compass of sun
Is contained, what sealed apparitions of summer,
What transfixed ambulations. If you could cut
Right to the heart and uncouple the innermost rings
Beyond those nerves you would see the structure of air.

Lazarus

Finally (in this dream) the Roman
Thrust his sword right through me.
I woke upon a pain which would not go.

It would be futile to describe the days
That followed, to talk of flame and fever,
Of red-hot irons and the like:

I was on fire with pain. I bore it badly.
They gave me cordials of blue-flowering
Borage but the fever would not break.

The last time I came round the pain had gone:
Then, after the long night, at dawn
The window blurred back into darkness.

I know you would have me tell you
Of spirits standing in white groves to meet me,
Of staircases ascending to the skies,

But that I cannot do. I have grown old
With the bandage-marks still on me.
They show me what I was and what I will be.

As you go home you will think, "Death's secret
Was not his because he was not destined
Yet to be dead". I cannot say.

I only knew of nothing and that, too,
Was of the world. I limp in the sun
Knowing that other. Darkness has its right.

His cry that ripped me out of nothing
By my roots, calling my name, that brought me
Back to the spectre of the light,

That cry, I hear it still in sleep.
I come awake, but paralysed, my arms
Imprisoned in the sheet, my legs rigid,

Unshivering cold. Sleep-walkers move
Without waking. I wake and cannot move.
How long this lasts again I cannot tell you,

A moment or an hour. It passes when I hear
Voices, long silent, in the courtyard saying,
As once they did, "Lazarus, yes, Lazarus".

Notes to a Suicide

I

Act Five, Scene Five: who is there left
To care? *Exeunt omnes*, barely alive. But no,
Not *omnes*, there's one still lying there
Just visible as the lights are faded.

Which one? The one who worked hard
Not to smile; who, when he did, had better
Teeth than any. That was him, the young one
With a heart like a snared drum.

Who else could it have been, given
The circumstance? He was the man
Who refused to initial the armistice,
Who turned guerrilla when the war was won.

That was the way he was. When he was briefly
The central figure he moved, stumbling, aside;
And when he had lines he stepped quickly
Downstage and mumbled. But our eyes

Followed him to the door. He had the last laugh,
It seemed to him at the time; his dreams
Were of silence. Why will no one come
To drag off his body now that he has the floor?

2

There is an endless succession of rooms
To which you are not admitted. Not that I look
For you every day, you would have none of that.
You are the total of all closed books.

I see you, from above (an aerial shot
You composed yourself), walking into the sea,
Waving. There comes a moment when
Only your hand can be seen above the waves,

Then you are gone, all of you. Once
You meant this as a joke, the only truth.
There is no way to return out of the sea.
This film cannot be run backwards.

Why, then, do I care? Most of the time
You had not much room for pleasantness.
Your industry was geared for the sharp manufacture
Of what most mistook for deliberate mistakes.

Illuminations of the Letter O

I

Brocade and embellishment
At the round boundary, a garland,
A gold-leaf beating of bounds
About the parish of snow:

Transfixed in wading the white acres,
Jailed in his pretty prison,
The subject of the text he cannot walk in
Is the sole occupant of zero;

Except for a statutory decorative bird
In permanent and stilled migration
Towards what words there are,
Yet mute when the darkness closes.

Between the snow and the page
Lies the matrix of the world,
But buried deep and inaccessible
As the mystery of the margin.

Shepherd seeking out sheep, probing
With his staff, examining the drift
Before him, or hunter trudging the line
Of hidden traps (for he is one or other),

A guest under grey heaven, one day he'll step
Into another meaning. Meanwhile he awaits
The coming of others to witness the poised
Mirage of angels over blank fields.

2

Of nothing and of wonder; of a line
Returning to the point where it began;
And all conjoined, three in a single token
Of zero and of joy and of no end:

Under unfathomable, regretless heaven
Dance in a round ring, syllables, your feet
Returning to the place of other dancers,
Nothing and dancing making the balance even.

Singing of burned-out suns, gaze yet again
Into the eyes of children passing,
Whose every glance reiterates the wise
Shape of all things and of nothing, the division,

The circumstance that brief breath brings us to.
Move seasons, die, unwind the endless coil
Of my unknowing; and when that same unknowing
Drops into nothing, give it its true name.

Right Time

The tall clock still stands still
In the front hall, truly
My grandfather's clock. I inherited
His lost pulse and his receipt
For it. Now both seem small.

Its pendulum was stopped, its undernourished
Note given silence for every mortal
Illness in the house I was born in.
Its face saw out our lives;
Quarters, halves, the elaborate

Small joys and pains and sub-divisions,
Moment by gently-jolted moment,
Exemplaries of love, so softly then
As though they might disturb unwillingly
Another in luck in the next room.

A slowly-ageing present tense
Of nameless stars, which out of a brief
Clouding acquire a colder glance,
And yet with their thin snowlight
Alive not blankly timeless:

So with my clock's gilt hands. They tell me
A meaningless hour. The painted town
Above them with its green sea and calm sky
Has a sun at never-midnight. The stone
Weights were lost when I brought them

To this place. That old man, who sang to me
The hymns of all his certainties,
He'd hang his cap on the top crude

Wooden pinnacle on the high crown
Of this clock-case; every eighth day

Hoist the next eight with his black key
And be content. He and buried farms
Talk to me through the fled arithmetic
Behind these arbitrary numerals. This silence
Is true company, the painted sands speak.

Boundaries

A black flag giving assent to spring's
Illumination of the book of hours,
The whiteness of my almond tree; in anthracite
Of feathers, this blackbird singing.

Each evening just before dusk, in festival,
His pertinent cadenza to the day
Defines his territory, marks his boundary
Under my work-room window. The pane,

A yard or two of air, that's all there is
Between us. All? Yellow flute, black performer,
He flaunts his beginner's luck, chiding, gliding
Through variations upon unfound themes;

His musical unconcern crucial
To the seeming accident of song,
His obbligato signature deriving
From ancestries of whistling, unanimous

With the blossom. He, hero of branches,
(Trick of his head) perpetually surprised
To be trapped inside what he whistles,
Inventing nothing, being invention,

Flawless as makes no matter, taunting me
To delight. He essays yes out of his history
Against all configurations of silence
Through the one throat he happens to have.

Evening adjusts the trance of sky. His spate
Of acrobatics on a three-line stave,
Sardonic, repetitious, can never be whole
Except as part of what I wish to be whole.

Music to him is custom. His easy tricks
Are my despair. I turn back to the page
Where my chantepleure is born already broken.
What can I bid against him but misère?

And yet the future is still to be done.
He stabs me broad awake with notes
Not of his whistling. Thus runs spring's rigmarole
With no song substitute for any other.

Tune for a Celestial Musician

Too long in deference to the dark
We have supposed alert and dulcet
Devices, acquired by private miracle,
Were his, making his music oracle;

That passing the open door of his studio
In the sky we should see him swinging in space,
That disguising our tears we should cry,
"Play it again, Sam Angel, play it again".

Why? Were his five-finger exercises on breath
Better than ours? Are the more distant stars
His sounding-board? Must we assume a form
Always beyond us rankles to music in him?

No, he is ours; and ours his repertoire
Of stances. We dreamed his execution
Out of our fear of silence. Morning after morning
Sees him die as midnight after midnight

Re-invents him. Bring down his instrument
From the clouds; lute, lyre, whatever it is
He holds, with each impossible string.
His tune is of our own imagining.

Homing Pigeons

Out of a parsimony of space unclenched,
Into the not known and yet familiar,
They ascend out of their hunger, venture
A few tentative arcs, donate new
Circumflexions to the order of strange sky;
Then blend to a common tangent and so render
Themselves to the essence of what they are.

What beguilement shepherds the heart home?
Not what we know but some late lode-stone
Which, far, was always there, drawing us
To a meaning irreducible, to a fixed star.

Why then the falling, all the fumbling
As tumbler pigeons, fools flying, with the most
Inept of masteries? But flying still
And, despite awkwardness, being, as best we can,
Committed, in the chance weather we approach,
To what and where, without a sense of reward,
We may reach and trust to be fed.

A Lost Word

In certain lights when the eyes, not seeking
Truth or effect, sometimes not even looking
Properly, see unfamiliar faces reveal
How they were long ago, young, fragile, special even,
Or predict, occupied with some thought,
Doubtless of no consequence, which ages them,
How they will look ten or twenty years hence;

And when sounds which seem on the brink
Of augury hold back, a near gale from nowhere
Dismantling the house on a cloudless summer midnight;
Or when, alone, just as coals collapse in the grate,
One hears footsteps on bare boards in the carpeted room
Above and then a voice, unanswering now, from where
It called and a shadow moved on the stairs;

One cannot escape the feeling that something
Almost at hand eludes us, that characters imprinted
On the other side of a page, in parallel, press through
On what we are trying to say, and would disclose
News or perhaps solace, some almost obvious
Simple sentence which would complete
The heart's short story of magnificence.

It would be good to believe that those strange faces
Were known once, loved maybe; that if we could find
The upstairs walkers hiding in a wardrobe
Or some cupboard and tease them from their silly shame
At being found, that stammering with surprise
At being discovered at all, or from long silence,
Unsure of their lines, they would give us the lost word.

Unable to sleep, shaving at half-dawn,
Unwilling to gaze full into the eyes
Of the latest forgery in the bathroom mirror,
Today's bad copy of an earlier work,
I have no lust for secrets. It is enough that the blade
Is sharp, that the sun lurks then rises over my garden's
Blown roses and its brown turmoil of leaves.

The Piano Tuner

Every six months his white stick brings him,
Punctilious to the minim stroke of nine
On the day we dread. Edgy at his knock,
We infuse a grudging warmth into voices
Asking his health, attempt to ease
His coat from him, which courtesy he refuses;

And usher him to the instrument. He entrusts
Us with nothing, disdains, from his black tent,
Our extended hands where the awkward staircase
Bends, rattles the banisters with his bag,
Crabs past the chairs. Finally at the keyboard
He discharges quick arpeggios of judgement.

"As I expected," he says, dismissing us;
And before we close the door excludes us
Further, intent in his flummox of strange tools
And a language beyond us. He begins to adjust
And insist on the quotients and ratios
Of order in encased reverberant wire.

All morning, then, downstairs we cower;
The thin thunder of decibels, octaves slowly
Made absolute, which will not break into storm,
Dividing us from him. The house is not the same
Until long after he leaves, having made one thing
Perfect. "Now play," say his starched eyes.

Among Friends

The cloud of clear wine, each questioning
Harmonious; even secrets of the spirit
Given up, ifs and buts gone quite soon
After the last of the third carafe.
Then what? The resurrection of seems,
Nightmare, daymare, whatever further hours
Haunt clockwork, eat at our fretwork meaning.
Then we come down to the intolerance
Of our dreams and what might pass for dreams
Given the safeguards of illusion,
Drops in the last goblet. Was there ever
Such red, such dusty taste of brief sun,
So near, so unfading? This done,
That done, drinking — how else? — alone,
I signal to you over an empty glass.
So the strict seasons pass,
So the strict seasons run.

Note Found on a Mantelpiece

Welcome: the house greets you, is yours
For as long as you're able to stay,
Somewhere or other here
There are most things you'll require
From improvised day to day.
We have our special places
For this and that, of course,
But don't be bound by them. And, yes,
There *are* secrets lying about
In the backs of the darker drawers.
If you happen to come on one
Don't feel a guilty guest;
Let it be yours, too,
If you should wish it so, and can
Decipher it. It won't be missed.
There are others so well hidden
We're surprised ourselves when they fall
From behind a shelf or wherever...
Please help yourself in the garden.
Nothing's forbidden.
Upstairs, the big bed's best.
There are no noises in the night
As far as we're aware (unless
You've brought your own,
Some nightmare or poltergeist),
Except for the chimes in the hall,
Foreshadowing doom with their din.
No doubt you'll get not to hear them
Just when you've settled in,
As your time runs out and you're going.

An Ending

Lady, so long since gone, I am in limbo
Between an instinct of the dark, the sense
My own unfinished time has brought me to
And what you said you saw, and seemed to see,
On your last day. Feeling the faint pang
Of expensive appetite which, it appears,
Grates in the dying, you sent me running
For chicken and champagne. A whim, a delusion
Of hunger, that's all it was. When I returned
You saw things which I could not see.

"Aren't the flowers dark?" you said
Of the four yellow chrysanthemums which exploded
Pom-poms of formal light in silence
Under the black beams of that living-room
Turned sick-room; the ceiling the floor, too,
Of the empty room above in which you were born.

No one, I think now, could have invented
Such death-bed syllables. For then you said
(The poisoned, visionary words
Falling into the place of shining,
The chest of drawers, the cold brasses alive
At twitching firelight, the ticking clock
By the chimney stilled for your sleeping,
This place of much of your living
Which you had cleaned — how often? —
With cloth and polish and broom),
"I can see dust on everything".

But far away you were gliding into a long beyond
Of snows, of future weather's total indifference,
Of your own uncaring. I held you in my arms
As you were dying, with no sense then of a need,
As now, which would ask, *Why, where, these words*
From one so prosaic, so afraid of any ending?

Then you'd return with small apologies;
The sliced white chicken-breast unwanted,
The wine, in a kitchen cup to disguise
This once in a poor lifetime's last libation,
Spurned, too. Again, in shadows of shadows,
Which I believed you saw, you perceived not ease
But some uncounted-on and unaccountable
Glimpse of a pleasantness which made you say,
You who had been so afraid of your own eyes' closing
(Too easily persuaded, so I thought, of the goodness
Of this death — yet, was there someone there
Whose known gaze met your own?), "Well, well, well,
What a surprise, what a surprise".

At last, in my arms still, those far snows
Finally kept you. The rituals done,
We stayed that night in the house alone together.
Neighbours fussed, grudgingly left us
Each with the other. I had no fear, mother.

And it was in my waking that I heard them,
My neighbours making up their morning fires
On either side. In the same world as them
I went down into the day that they and I would wear,
The winter sun's new garment. Into the room where you lay
I entered, took back the sheet from your face
And, without grief, grateful for your easy going,
Gave you the token of the love you were aware
No longer of, the kiss you could not share.

Forgive me for what happened then.
My lips upon your forehead tasted the foul grave
And I spat it to my hand and rushed
To wash the error from my proud flesh.

There There, Then

So, to a child sobbing
Following some petty fall.
There seems hardly a graze
But white with hurt a rasp burns,
Real though barely visible,
After such little distance down.

Does he then need to be told
That no huge damage is done?
No, rather murmured to
That (There there, then)
All's not irreparable,
That the world may restart

If breath's not held-back,
Hugged-back so precariously,
Refused as though for minutes
Before the next breath's taken;
That the shaken frame finds ways
Of healing injury that's none.

But why, child, why the fall?
Ah, it's useless to say
That that's a grave, bottomless notion
And all to do, in the end,
With gravity. The real pain,
Which cannot be exhaled,

Churns unexplained, is more
Than half-imagined. It lodges,
And was perhaps discovered
(And how old was the child?)
After such falling in the feigned
Mildness of a garden where the stones,

Sharp for the first time, chose
Edges at that instant of descent.
It's no help now to suppose
That, when the first tree grew
Up from the seed of nothing,
No hurt, no mortal harm was meant.

Where Else?

Where else is there to sing
Save where we are?
True that the imperfect bone,
Stricken with undefinable complaint,
Some slight flaw in the root
For which new spring and summer,
Proliferating, cannot compensate,
Is not the topmost nor the perfect place;
But here it is, accessible,
Not broken yet nor fallen.
It is the boundary at the utmost edge
Of what we have. Whatever note,
Shaken from our frames, goes out,
As when a thrush sings late
Into the renewal of dusk
Which is not his or ours,
The known's not only what the heart
Treasures, hungry for great privilege.

Keep close, keep close. In the night, dearest,
Frontiers are unobserved. Sentries
With no vast care, except for sleep,
Also unsafe, shoot into shadows. And the law is
(Drastic ill-luck) that their bullets
Wilfully go straight to the target
Of what's invisible by day. They stop
The phrase which was about to say, almost
Like a hair touching one's face,
Something of song, perhaps of the true
Nature of song; of how fragment and grace-note
Would be resolved with the next dawn-chorus,
Except that, silence now, the heart's hit.

As it Happens

The ones whose images came unbidden
Into me, brow, jaw-line and shoulder-stoop,
Whose faces I shave daily; the long-hidden
Similarities seen more surely later, the whole crop:

I have them and take them all, having no choice,
If not exactly gladly, vaguely seeing
The sediments of my bedrock there to be rejoiced in,
There being no alternative to being.

Waiting in the Garden

If down into the green glaze
Of this evening garden suddenly cascaded
No less than angels, having been first
White hesitations, a small suggestion of cloud,
Then raggedly spiralling, trying to find formation,
Finally falling to be material, wingtip feathers
Transparent alabaster;

The beginners, good boys killed on their motorbikes,
In novices' nightshirts, shaming
The smiling patriarchs — who died before
The Bible was set down — as they clip
The tops of the lilac-trees, crash-landing a-clatter
In the rhubarb, snapping the stems off short,
Breaking their legs yet again.

What would I say if the aged, approaching,
Rubbing their shins, uttered "Come",
And then repeated it, "Come, come. We come to take you
To where the secret is"? Of course, I would ask
For their credentials; and they'd produce
From inside zipped-up pockets the required
Flying licences, innoculation forms and gilt IDs;

The old white-parsley-bearded flight-lieutenants
Delving for scuffed quill-written jobs
On parchment. They'd begin: *We the Archangel Gabriel,*
Foreign Secretary of Heaven, Request and Require...
And then their images, illuminated, faded Byzantine,
Their Wing-Commander, meanwhile, smiling a small smile,
Remembering how many abortive sorties he's flown.

And the young, the latest-risen from cooling blood,
Presenting their baffled grins from postage stamps
Of pictures taken in booths in the far corners
Of celestial Woolworths. You can see them jostling,
Fussing their hair, finessing with gold combs,
Crowding for next turn, excited. Smile, flash,
Smile, flash, 2, 3, 4. The curtain then drawn back,

And then the waiting.
What answer do they bring?
What answer not yet given by the evening light
And the questions and pleasantnesses
At the table in the green of this lady's garden?
And the strong white house, its books and pictures,
The questions and children I have pondered in it?

Would my most welcome visitors, awkwardly ascending
From their failed mission, be stripped
Of their silver stripes, be Heaven-bound not grounded,
Confined to base, forfeit their harps? I'd hope not.
Poor lucky souls, knowing the mystery.
I'd signal them "Good luck,
Good flying" as the garden darkened.

Turning

When would winter end?
The numb garden lay sentenced
In frost, all green long gone to ground,
As day by day, hour by grudging hour,
The birds grew fewer.
Day by day the trees thinned and darkened.
When would winter end?

Threats perched as strangers
In hawthorn and apple tree,
Magpies, unwelcome black and white
Patchwork, to be clapped away;
Even a sparrow-hawk perched, lurking,
As the solstice could not be
Coaxed on by the ritual of crumbs.
When would winter end?

Then the clenched earth relented
And there where there had been nothing
Crouched three winter aconites, each
With five yellow fingertips drawn close
(A poised Italianate gesture), savouring
The sun; and then, surprised,
The crocuses' audacity, blue
Under the frost-burned rose-bush.
And winter's long watch was ended
Insomuch as each moment then
Hurried to the truth of March.

Evening in the Square

The swifts are invisibly mending the sky
Where last night's wind tore it to pieces,
Stitching, delirious with light labour,
High on it, with dizzy double-darning
Done in twos. Such work's a tall order.

Clearly up there everything's still in tatters,
Total anarchy, a right old tangle,
All in each other's way. This lot need better
Management, a good union. But they are natural
Non-joiners, although they're fellow-travellers.

Darker. They're frantic with deadline screeches.
They'll never finish. The pigeons line
The high eaves, baffled. Get an agent for this show,
Do it with ribbons: a fortune. I'd do it myself
But mine is, alas, only a poet's licence.

Storm

Thunder. Unlatch the front door and the back
For bolts to pass through without hindrance.

Lightning. Turn mirrors to the wall
Lest it stop to admire itself and then kill.

First, shunting of iron trucks in the sky, then
The flickering blast-furnaces tapped briefly open.

Four million iron bedsteads angrily thrown out;
Where will the Roman gods lie down to-night?

Chests of drawers shifted in all the mansions
Of heaven, every single floorboard ripped up,

A millenium of free coal going down tin cellars,
Calamities of guilt burying zinc sheds,

All eternity's ripe walnuts being cracked in two;
The impossible silver decisions, the last judgement.

Now the late bullets of executioner's rain,
The end of the world has come, and we but children.

We cannot hide in the cupboard under the stairs
With old coats over our heads, dusty and musty,

Counting the seconds. The sky is in charge,
The mirrors are blind, and the swifts stopped.

Tuscan Cypresses

Black-green, green-black, unbending intervals
On far farm boundaries; all years are one to them.
Their noon stillness is beyond decipherment.
They are at the beginning and end of the heart's quandaries.

On the darkest night roadside they judge the earth's turning,
On hills the brightness of stars is the brightness of day.
Each like a young bride is awake at too-soon dawn and
      hurrying midnight,
Yet each, like every death, is uncaring, each unknown.

They stand like heretics over long-decayed churches.
Some single as lepers are doomed to keep watch alone.
Fell those single ones, blast out their roots and detonate
Your only certainty; the curse upon you is whole.

They are the silences between the notes Scarlatti left
      unwritten,
The silence after the last of Cimarosa's fall.
They are all seasons, they are every second of time.
They do not improvise, all is in strict measure.

Though they reach to the impossible they never outgrow
Or deceive themslves, being nothing but what they are;
They know nothing of angels only of the enticement of hills.
They look down on lakes, the persuasive sea's vainglory.

They have seen the waters divide for divinities
But that was long ago so now peace possesses them;
Their only restlessness is the need for great annexations;
They would come into their inheritance by black growth and
      stealth.

They march over the border down into Umbria;
Their uniform gives no glint of the sunlight back.
As the gun-carriages threaten by they are the darkness
Of future suicides and firing-squads ahead.

Their solemnity is of Umbria, of burnt earth.
Even they do not know the bottom of it all, the last
Throw of the dice, the black rejoicing, the dying,
The vegetable lie, the audacity of bright flowers.

They barely respond to the stark invention of storms.
Enemies of the living light, they are Dido's lament.
They grow in the mind, haunting, the straight flames
Of fever, black fire possessing the blood.

They have stood at the edges of all events, rehearsed
Vergil's poems before he was born, awaited his death
In another country. Only the oldest of oaks can converse
       with them
In the tentative syllables of their patient language.

Lorenzo stood among them as the black-scarved women
Buried a child under cold, motionless candlelight,
The red banners of death and the white surplices.
Lorenzo would die soon, wasted, his wife gripping his ankle.

Are they the world's memorial, its endless throng
Of tombstones? Are they the existence of light before it was
       born?
That aloofness, that uncaring of what is and what is not:
Are they all spent grief at knowing no knowing?

They do not recognise this given world from another,
Having watched Adam and Eve limp from the Garden,
The serpent ingratiate itself into the world's only apple tree,
The silver rivers of Eden begin their grey tarnish.

130

They are the trustees and overseers of absentee landlords,
Keeping a black account of the generations of thin, uneasy
    labourers.
They withhold judgements and watch traditions die,
Are unrejoicing over the wedding party dances.

They have watched man and woman lie down in their vows,
    and wake
Into happiness made new by morning,
And observed the *contadini* setting out for the yellow fields,
Not caring whether they should return or not return.

They watched the Great Death blacken the land,
Agnolo di Tura del Grasso, sometimes called The Fat,
Bury his five children with his own two hands,
And many another likewise, the grave-diggers dying

Or running, knowing of more than death, into the hills.
There death stood waiting between the cypresses.
The terraces of vine and olive retched with the weight of
    their dying.
The terraces crumbled and the new famine began.

The cypresses stood over it all in the putrefaction
Of silence; silence of chantings dead in the priests' throats;
Silence of merchant and beggar, physician and banker,
Of silversmith and wet-nurse, mason and town-crier.

The cypresses stood over it all and watched and watched;
You could not call this enmity, it is the world's way.
Their stance seems set as though by ordinance and yet it is
    not.
It is merely the circumstance of the mystery, the reason for
    churches.

They are not everything, but they are trees.
They watch the pulse in heaven of cold stars
And the common smoke gone up from the body's burning,
They know the sourness of vinegar,

The sweetness and smiling of holy wine,
But they partake of neither in spirit;
Cannot be bribed into turning away, not even briefly.
There is no buying off their vigilance.

They are the melancholy beyond explaining,
Beyond belief. Accepting this, they are not tempted
To put on more than their little green.
Theirs is the dark of the unbelieving, the unknowing, the
    darkness of pits.

Some few are deformed, though fewer
That in their multitudes and assembling legions
Their particles might have been heir to.
From birth their spines are erect, their outlines the essence of
    given symmetry.

Departure from this is brief aberration;
They must look down from their own escarpments of air, the
    wild lilies beneath them,
The wild mignonette, the dog-rose unheeded.
If they could smile a gale would storm south over Africa.

Each one is the containment of every one there was,
A compounding of all cypresses, of all their stillness.
They are the elegant dancers who never dance,
Preferring to watch the musicians, the bustling ones.

They are trees, but they are more than trees,
They go deeper than that. They are at the heart

Of the ultimate music; the poor loam and Roman melody of
     Keats's body
Sings silently beneath them.

What will there be of them when all men are gone?
No one to witness the seed of their secret cones,
The deep black seed, the seed beginning in Eden, coming
     from nothing,
From the beginning falling in Eden.

Only they can tell of that old story and they are silent
For all the long wisdoms have passed into them;
So silence, since it all comes to nothing.
See how it all burns, all, in the black flames of their silence,
     their silence, untelling.

V

Several Episodes Reported with No Offence Meant to God

1. Sunday Morning Lie-in

On the seventh day he lay down
In a corner of what he had made,
Whatever it was. The place where he dropped,
Numb from his labour, was a desert,
The rubble and this and that of the builder's yard.
And now he was oblivion. He was night.

"Which way?" There came a voice,
That of a holy man, a long time later,
Seeking the god's face, asking
The emptiness of the wilderness,

"Which way?" Endlessly piteous, the mewling
Shifted sand that had silted the god's ears.
His elbows to his head, the god turned over
As mountain chains rose up and the earth shook.

Again, again, "Which way? Which the true way?"
The voice in its own torment
Until the god relented. For the first time
And the last the god spoke.

Go away, I do not hear you. Let me sleep.
Know I am deaf. Know that when I began
To make what stands about you
I gave away my hearing, dispersed it among men.
You ask me the true way.
Go and ask men.

2. Poste Restante, Counter Closed

The terrible noise of the first thunder,
The noise of something enormous
Crashing from quite a height.
So the god looked down from a particularly
Distant place he had constructed. He decided
That even the noise of unimportant fallings
Could divert him in his loneliness.
The noise was the noise of Adam leaving Eden
Without a forwarding address.

3. Entropy Revisited

The second law of thermodynamics
Discovered by some clever dicks
Who should have known better than
To report their findings in *Nature*
Was not exactly as god intended
It to turn out. All that bit
About matter moving from order
Towards further disorder gave god a shock
To read it in cold print.
Not what I meant, he said
Not at all what I meant.

Nobody heard him. Atoms tore apart,
Breaking their hearts. Chaos
Began to reign in the firmament.

A man with a violin
And a heavy moustache listened
As a train on a nearby railway

Hooted in passing and, passing,
Changed its note.
The notion of time came forth
And was duly mute.

4. Quo Vadis?

God got lost on his way home,
No one to tell him the way, of course.
No use asking man.
He suffered a tiny pang of remorse;
Another million galaxies were born.

5. Song of Anti-Matter

Oh dear, what can this matter be?
It's all right here in a negative galaxy,
But elsewhere, on the wrong side of symmetry, shatters me.
    Positrons always play fair.

Do not confuse me with black holes at large
In the graveyard of stars, the whirlpools that gorge
Events to non-happening. My opposite charge
    Is gratis, electric and free.

And when I collide with my sister, real matter,
We both disappear with a hell of a clatter,
Which tends to prove god is as mad as a hatter,
    And our E is the square of mc.

But neutrons, electrons and protons at play,
When it comes to the end, the last cinders of clay,
And the cosmos collapses, I might get my way
    And flare a new infinity.

Oh dear, what can this matter be?
Being a part of the universe flatters me.
But I'm real, a kind of invisible Battersea,
    See me or not I am there.

6. Ode to Winston Place

Hail to thee, Winston Place,
Former Lancashire cricketer,
Decorous at the crease;
Who, upon retirement,
Became an umpire;
But retired from this, too,
Finding it obnoxious
To give people out.

God, in your utmost hiding-place,
Let this man be a lesson to you.

Soliloquy of a Secret Policeman

I am so gentle in my questioning
They hardly murmur as I hit them;
They proffer me blood in gratitude.

I show them true black in the muzzle
Of my gun. Nothing is darker than
The night trained under my sight.

We're a gentle family. My wife is proud of me,
(In the darkness of our bed her body is white);
"I believe in plenty of rope," she whispers softly.

I wake in the whiteness of our room,
Then flex before the mirror. Happy the man
Who goes to work with the bright prospect of pleasure.

It was not always easy. Once I sat
In the back of an armoured car shooting at children,
Jolted so much I could hardly hit them.

But I hit enough — and this was noticed
In the appropriate quarter (there is a justice);
I was promoted to Assistant Torturer.

The techniques are boring, and by now
Well-known. You will have seen
The basic handbook in the new edition.

My wife shows the neighbours the illustrations
Of me at work in the coloured pages;
The best are silver-framed on the piano.

Since we were told that the high readings
On the electric meters in the cellars
Mean nothing, I drive home with an easy mind.

Our rubber truncheons are dry-cleaned
Regularly. In the canteen I tremble under the glance
Of the admiring waitress with black lashes.

God has a strange sense of beneficence
(God, forgive me for that, but I have learned
That it is true). Was He trying — what futility —

To give them us as gift to compensate
Them for coming out wrong from His Holy Wash,
And this glorious country to be held in trust for us

Until we could arrive? Their future lies
In Education. Look, I can count up to six
On my revolver. She's a beauty, black, blank,

Black in the muzzle. Each time I take her out
For the evening, she smiles and blows kisses
In all directions, always asking for more.

Under whose hand will she lie after my death?
I have bequeathed her in my will. If my will's
Disputed, oh we shall be buried

In separate graves, my dear gun and I.
Dying, my regret will be
I did not do more to educate the children.

They hunger for the future. Oh, I dream
It will teach them the bloody alphabet
And to count One Two Three Four Five Six.